Your Lifelong Bible Guide for Every Stage of Life

- ♥ Thoughtfully curated for children, teens, adults, and seniors
- ♥ Covers real-life situations and spiritual needs across all seasons of life
- ♥ Organized into 50+ meaningful topics for practical guidance and inspiration

Yesudas Solomon

WOG BOOKS 187

First Edition 2025

Author:

Yesudas Solomon

Published By:

Bible Minutes, www.WordOfGod.in

Copyright: Public Domain

This book is not copyright protected. You are free to download, print and make copies without any permission from us.

Download:

www.WordOfGod.in and www.Archive.org

Contact Us:

WhatsApp: +91 7676505599
Email: wordofgod@wordofgod.in

Contents

Foreword

The Bible is more than a collection of ancient texts—it is a timeless guide, offering wisdom, encouragement, and strength for every stage of life. Whether you are a child learning to trust God, a teenager navigating relationships and personal growth, an adult seeking wisdom and purpose, or a senior reflecting on life's deeper truths, Scripture provides direction and clarity.

This book is carefully structured to help individuals across all generations walk in faith, grow spiritually, and live according to God's will. No matter where you are on life's journey, the verses within these pages will serve as a steadfast companion, offering guidance when no one else is there to help.

Here's a brief overview of what you will find in each section:

* **Kids:** Verses that teach love for God, obedience to parents, kindness, honesty, and using good words to encourage others.
* **Teens:** Foundational principles for faith, honoring parents, personal conduct, purity, wisdom, and navigating relationships with integrity.
* **Adults:** Guidance on maintaining faith, developing wisdom, shaping character, strengthening relationships, fulfilling purpose in work, and persevering through life's challenges.

* **Seniors (50+):** Scriptures focused on wisdom, faith, peace, contentment, mentorship, leaving a legacy, and preparing for eternity with confidence and hope.

Rooted in the principle of **Matthew 10:8, "Freely you have received; freely give,"** this book is offered entirely free, **without copyright restrictions**. Whether for personal, commercial, or non-commercial use, it can be shared, studied, or distributed without limitation.

May these verses inspire, uplift, and strengthen you as you walk in faith, grow in wisdom, and seek God's presence in every step of life's journey.

Yesudas Solomon
3-Jun-2025

1. Heavenly guide for Kids

100+ Bible Verses Every Child Should Know

1.1. Loving & Trusting God

This list of Bible verses emphasizes foundational truths about our relationship with God, encouraging love, trust, worship, and communication with Him. It begins with the greatest commandment—loving God with all our heart—and continues by teaching us to trust Him fully, especially in times of fear. The verses remind us that our love for God is a response to His great love for us, shown most clearly through Jesus. Believing in Jesus and obeying His teachings are essential acts of faith and love.

Prayer, praise, and thanksgiving are recurring themes, showing that our relationship with God involves ongoing communication and joyful worship. The verses highlight God's goodness, His never-ending love, and His role as our caring Shepherd. They also affirm that God loves all people deeply and desires our worship and trust. Altogether, these Scriptures offer a simple but powerful guide for living a life that honors and enjoys God.

1. **Love God most!**
   "Love the Lord your God with all your heart..." - Mark 12:30

2. **Trust God always**
   "Trust in the LORD with all your heart..." - Proverbs 3:5

3. **Trust God when you're scared**

   "When I am afraid, I put my trust in you." - Psalm 56:3

4. **Love God because He loves you**

   "We love because he first loved us." - 1 John 4:19

5. **Believe in Jesus**

   "...Believe in the Lord Jesus, and you will be saved..." - Acts 16:31

6. **Show you love Jesus by obeying Him**

   "If you love me, keep my commands." - John 14:15

7. **Remember God's words**

   "I have hidden your word in my heart that I might not sin against you." - Psalm 119:11

8. **Talk to God often**

   "Pray continually," - 1 Thessalonians 5:17

9. **Praise God!**

   "Let everything that has breath praise the LORD. Praise the LORD." - Psalm 150:6

10. **Be happy about God!**

    "Shout for joy to the LORD, all the earth." - Psalm 100:1

11. **Thank God because He is good**
"Give thanks to the LORD, for he is good; his love endures forever." - Psalm 118:1

12. **God's love never stops**
"Give thanks to the LORD, for he is good. His love endures forever." - Psalm 136:1

13. **Remember God is love**
"...God is love." - 1 John 4:8

14. **God loves everyone so much**
"For God so loved the world that he gave his one and only Son..." - John 3:16

15. **Show God you are happy!**
"Clap your hands, all you nations; shout to God with cries of joy." - Psalm 47:1

16. **(Similar to Mark 12:30) - Reinforces loving God completely**
"Love the LORD your God with all your heart and with all your soul and with all your strength." - Deuteronomy 6:5

17. **Worship only God**
"...Worship the Lord your God, and serve him only." - Matthew 4:10

18. Worship the God who made us

"Come, let us bow down in worship, let us kneel before the LORD our Maker;" - Psalm 95:6

19. Give your worries to God because He cares

"Cast all your anxiety on him because he cares for you." - 1 Peter 5:7

20. God takes care of me like a shepherd

"The LORD is my shepherd, I lack nothing." - Psalm 23:1

1.2. Obeying Parents & Grown-ups

This collection of verses emphasizes the importance of listening to, respecting, and obeying parents and other trusted leaders. Children are encouraged to honor their father and mother, not only because it is right, but because it pleases God. The Bible repeatedly highlights that wise children pay attention to the teachings and guidance of their parents and elders, showing that obedience and respect are lifelong values.

Beyond the family, the verses also teach children to listen to godly leaders, such as teachers and pastors, and above all, to hear and obey God's Word. Obedience is not just about rules—it's about growing in wisdom, showing love and respect, and living a life that honors both God and those He has placed in authority. These verses offer a strong foundation for learning discipline, responsibility, and godly character.

1. **Obey your parents**
    "Children, obey your parents in the Lord, for this is right." - Ephesians 6:1

2. **Make God happy by obeying your parents**
    "Children, obey your parents in everything, for this pleases the Lord." - Colossians 3:20

3.   **Respect your Mom and Dad**
     "Honor your father and your mother..." - Exodus 20:12

4.   **Listen to what Mom and Dad teach you**
     "Listen, my son, to your father's instruction and do not forsake your mother's teaching." - Proverbs 1:8

5.   **Keep listening to your parents**
     "Listen to your father, who gave you life, and do not despise your mother when she is old." - Proverbs 23:22

6.   **Remember what your parents tell you**
     "My son, keep your father's command and do not forsake your mother's teaching." - Proverbs 6:20

7.   **Pay attention when grown-ups teach you**
     "Listen, my sons, to a father's instruction; pay attention and gain understanding." - Proverbs 4:1

8.   **It's good to listen to God and obey**
     "...Blessed rather are those who hear the word of God and obey it." - Luke 11:28

9.   **Listen to your leaders, like teachers or pastors**
     "Have confidence in your leaders and submit to their authority..." - Hebrews 13:17

10. **Wise kids listen to their parents**

    "A wise son heeds his father's instruction..." - Proverbs 13:1

1.3. Being Kind, Loving & Sharing

This group of Bible verses focuses on how we should treat others with love, kindness, and humility. At the heart of it is the command to love others as we love ourselves—a love that reflects God's own love for us. The verses encourage forgiveness, compassion, and putting others before ourselves. Whether it's through kind words, helpful actions, or simply sharing what we have, the Bible teaches that love must be shown through how we live and how we treat those around us.

The passages also highlight the importance of living in peace, being cheerful, and caring deeply for others' needs and feelings. We're called to be peacemakers, helpers, and encouragers—even toward those who may not treat us kindly. These verses remind us that love is more than a feeling; it's a way of life that honors God and brings blessing to others. Living this way helps build stronger, more caring communities and reflects the heart of God in everyday actions.

1. **Love others like you love yourself**
   "...'Love your neighbor as yourself.'" - Mark 12:31

2. **Love each other**
   "Dear friends, let us love one another, for love comes from God..." - 1 John 4:7

3. **Be kind and forgive others**
   "Be kind and compassionate to one another, forgiving each other..." - Ephesians 4:32

4. **Treat others how you want to be treated**
   "Do to others as you would have them do to you." - Luke 6:31

5. **Say nice things to help others**
   "Therefore encourage one another and build each other up..." - 1 Thessalonians 5:11

6. **Care about others**
   "Be devoted to one another in love. Honor one another above yourselves." - Romans 12:10

7. **Do good things for everyone**
   "...let us do good to all people..." - Galatians 6:10

8. **Don't be selfish**
   "Do nothing out of selfish ambition... Rather, in humility value others above yourselves," - Philippians 2:3

9. **Do everything with love**
   "Do everything in love." - 1 Corinthians 16:14

10. **Show love by what you do**

"Dear children, let us not love with words... but with actions..." - 1 John 3:18

11. **Try to be peaceful with everyone**
"If it is possible, as far as it depends on you, live at peace with everyone." - Romans 12:18

12. **Be happy and cheerful!**
"A cheerful heart is good medicine..." - Proverbs 17:22

13. **Be kind to those who need help**
"Whoever is kind to the poor lends to the LORD..." - Proverbs 19:17

14. **Share what you have**
"Share with the Lord's people who are in need. Practice hospitality." - Romans 12:13

15. **Be nice even if someone isn't nice to you**
"Do not repay evil with evil or insult with insult. On the contrary, repay evil with blessing..." - 1 Peter 3:9

16. **Try to help people get along**
"Blessed are the peacemakers, for they will be called children of God." - Matthew 5:9

17. **Remember to do good and share**

"And do not forget to do good and to share with others, for with such sacrifices God is pleased." - Hebrews 13:16

18. Care about how others feel

"...be like-minded, be sympathetic, love one another, be compassionate and humble." - 1 Peter 3:8

19. Be kind and forgiving

"Blessed are the merciful, for they will be shown mercy." - Matthew 5:7

20. Try to do right and love others

"Whoever pursues righteousness and love finds life, prosperity and honor." - Proverbs 21:21

1.4. Telling the Truth & Being Honest

These verses teach the importance of honesty, integrity, and doing what is right in God's eyes. Telling the truth is not just a good habit—it's something God values deeply. We're reminded to speak truthfully, avoid lying, and never deceive or steal from others. God is pleased when we are trustworthy, even with small things, and He takes joy in those who live honestly and righteously.

Living with integrity builds trust and leads to a secure, peaceful life. These Scriptures also show that God expects fairness in all our dealings and wants us to be people of truth. Being honest honors God, helps others trust us, and reflects His character in the world. Choosing honesty in every situation is a way to show love for God and respect for others.

1. **Always tell the truth**
   "...speak truthfully to your neighbor..." - Ephesians 4:25

2. **God wants you to be honest**
   "The LORD detests lying lips, but he delights in people who are trustworthy." - Proverbs 12:22

3. **Don't tell lies about others**
   "You shall not give false testimony..." - Exodus 20:16

4. **Don't lie**
   "Do not lie to each other..." - Colossians 3:9

5. **Don't steal or lie or deceive others**
   "'Do not steal. "'Do not lie. "'Do not deceive one another." - Leviticus 19:11

6. **Don't take things that aren't yours**
   "You shall not steal." - Exodus 20:15

7. **Be trustworthy even with small things**
   "Whoever can be trusted with very little can also be trusted with much..." - Luke 16:10

8. **Be fair**
   "The LORD detests dishonest scales, but accurate weights find favor with him." - Proverbs 11:1

9. **It's safe to do what's right**
   "Whoever walks in integrity walks securely, but whoever takes crooked paths will be found out." - Proverbs 10:9

10. **God likes it when we tell the truth**
    "LORD, who may dwell in your sacred tent? ... The one whose walk is blameless, who does what is righteous, who speaks the truth from their heart;" - Psalm 15:1-2

1.5. Using Kind Words

These verses highlight the power of our words and the importance of speaking with kindness, wisdom, and self-control. God calls us to use our words to build others up, not tear them down. Speaking gently, avoiding anger, and choosing words that are helpful and full of grace are all ways we can reflect God's love in our daily conversations. Even when it's tempting to speak harshly or respond quickly, the Bible encourages us to listen first and be slow to speak and slow to become angry.

The Scriptures also remind us that our words carry weight—what we say can bring healing or hurt. We're warned to avoid lies, gossip, and harmful speech, and instead be thoughtful and careful in how we speak. Sometimes, staying silent is even the wiser choice. Ultimately, since God hears every word we say, we are called to speak in ways that honor Him and show love and respect to others. Our words matter—so we should use them well.

1. **Use words that help others, not hurt them**
   "Do not let any unwholesome talk come out of your mouths, but only what is helpful..." - Ephesians 4:29

2. **Use nice words, not angry words**

"A gentle answer turns away wrath, but a harsh word stirs up anger." - Proverbs 15:1

3. **Listen more, talk less, don't get angry quickly**
"...Everyone should be quick to listen, slow to speak and slow to become angry," - James 1:19

4. **Don't say bad things or lies**
"Keep your tongue from evil and your lips from telling lies." - Psalm 34:13

5. **Talk kindly to others**
"Let your conversation be always full of grace..." - Colossians 4:6

6. **Kind words make people feel good**
"Gracious words are a honeycomb, sweet to the soul..." - Proverbs 16:24

7. **Sometimes it's wise to be quiet**
"Even fools are thought wise if they keep silent..." - Proverbs 17:28

8. **Be careful what you say**
"Those who guard their mouths and their tongues keep themselves from calamity." - Proverbs 21:23

9. **Your words are important, use them carefully**

"...The tongue is a small part of the body, but it makes great boasts." - James 3:5

10. **God hears everything we say**

"But I tell you that everyone will have to give account on the day of judgment for every empty word they have spoken." - Matthew 12:36

1.6. Doing What is Right & Wise

These verses encourage us to live thoughtful, purposeful lives that reflect God's goodness and truth. They remind us to focus our minds on what is right, pure, and lovely, and to do what is good—not just once, but consistently. Whether through our words, actions, or attitudes, we are called to let our lives shine so others can see God at work in us. Even from a young age, we're encouraged to remember our Creator, seek wisdom, and do everything to bring glory to God.

The passages also teach that what we do matters—our actions reflect who we are and shape how others see us. God's Word is our guide for living wisely, making good choices, and treating others well. We're reminded to choose good friends, ask God for help in our plans, and always do our best as if we're doing it for Him. Most importantly, these verses celebrate that God made each of us special and full of purpose, created by Him and for Him.

1. **Think about good things**
    "...whatever is true... noble... right... pure... lovely... admirable... think about such things." - Philippians 4:8

2. Do good things so others see God is good
"...let your light shine before others, that they may see your good deeds..." - Matthew 5:16

3. Do the good things you know you should do
"If anyone, then, knows the good they ought to do and doesn't do it, it is sin for them." - James 4:17

4. Keep doing good, don't stop!
"Let us not become weary in doing good..." - Galatians 6:9

5. Do what's fair, be kind, walk with God
"...To act justly and to love mercy and to walk humbly with your God." - Micah 6:8

6. People know you by what you do
"Even small children are known by their actions..." - Proverbs 20:11

7. Remember God while you are young
"Remember your Creator in the days of your youth..." - Ecclesiastes 12:1

8. Do everything to make God happy
"...whatever you do, do it all for the glory of God." - 1 Corinthians 10:31

9. Golden Rule - Treat others nicely!

"So in everything, do to others what you would have them do to you..." - Matthew 7:12

10. **For parents, but teaches kids learning is important**
"Start children off on the way they should go, and even when they are old they will not turn from it." - Proverbs 22:6

11. **Choose good friends and do good things**
"Blessed is the one who does not walk in step with the wicked..." - Psalm 1:1

12. **Ask God to help you be wise**
"If any of you lacks wisdom, you should ask God..." - James 1:5

13. **Ask God to help with your plans**
"Commit to the LORD whatever you do, and he will establish your plans." - Proverbs 16:3

14. **God's Word helps us know the right way**
"Your word is a lamp for my feet, a light on my path." - Psalm 119:105

15. **God helps us learn**
"For the LORD gives wisdom; from his mouth come knowledge and understanding." - Proverbs 2:6

16. **Listen carefully when learning about God**

"Guard your steps when you go to the house of God. Go near to listen rather than to offer the sacrifice of fools..." - Ecclesiastes 5:1

17. God made you special!

"I praise you because I am fearfully and wonderfully made..." - Psalm 139:14

18. God made everything

"In the beginning God created the heavens and the earth." - Genesis 1:1

19. Jesus made everything

"Through him all things were made; without him nothing was made that has been made." - John 1:3

20. Do your best in everything, like you're doing it for God

"Whatever you do, work at it with all your heart, as working for the Lord..." - Colossians 3:23

1.7. Good Attitudes & Actions

These verses focus on developing strong character and a godly attitude in everyday life. They encourage us to be patient, self-controlled, and joyful, even in difficult situations. Rather than complaining, arguing, or giving in to anger, we're called to set a good example through our actions, words, and faith. Thinking about God and heavenly things helps us stay grounded and focused on what truly matters.

The Scriptures also teach us to love sincerely, hold tightly to what is good, and let the Holy Spirit grow qualities like kindness, patience, and self-control in our lives. When we rely on God, He helps us handle emotions wisely, overcome evil with good, and live with joy and peace. By choosing to live this way, we not only grow closer to God but also shine as positive examples for others to follow.

1. **Don't complain or argue**
    "Do everything without grumbling or arguing," - Philippians 2:14

2. **Be a good example**
    "...set an example... in speech, in conduct, in love, in faith and in purity." - 1 Timothy 4:12

3. **Choose to do good even when bad things happen**
    "Do not be overcome by evil, but overcome evil with good." - Romans 12:21

4. **It's good to be patient and have self-control**
    "Better a patient person than a warrior, one with self-control than one who takes a city." - Proverbs 16:32

5. **Think about God and heaven**
    "Set your minds on things above, not on earthly things." - Colossians 3:2

6. **Be patient, don't get angry fast**
    "Whoever is patient has great understanding, but one who is quick-tempered displays folly." - Proverbs 14:29

7. **It's okay to feel angry, but don't do wrong things because you're angry**
    "'In your anger do not sin'..." - Ephesians 4:26

8. **Ask God to help you for these**
    "But the fruit of the Spirit is love, joy, peace, forbearance [patience], kindness, goodness, faithfulness, gentleness and self-control." - Galatians 5:22-23

9. **Be happy in God**

   "Take delight in the LORD, and he will give you the desires of your heart." - Psalm 37:4

10. **Really love people. Hate bad things, hold on to good things**

    "Love must be sincere. Hate what is evil; cling to what is good." - Romans 12:9

2. Heavenly guide for Teens

100+ Bible Verses to Strengthen Faith & Identity

2.1. Relationship with God & Foundational Commands

These verses remind us that putting God first is the foundation of a faithful life. From the **Ten Commandments** to **Jesus' greatest commandment**, we are called to love God with all our heart, soul, mind, and strength. Worshiping only Him, honoring His name, keeping the Sabbath, and obeying His Word show our deep respect and devotion.

We're also encouraged to **trust in God's plan**, submit to His guidance, and resist evil. As we grow in faith, staying connected to God through **prayer, praise, and thanksgiving** becomes a daily joy. His Word becomes our compass — to meditate on, hide in our hearts, and live by.

The call is not just personal — it's outward too. Whether eating, working, or speaking, we're to **do everything in the name of Jesus and for God's glory**. Giving generously, gathering regularly with fellow believers, and making disciples worldwide are powerful ways we show our love for God in action.

In short: **Love God. Trust Him. Follow His ways. Share Him with others.**

Your Lifelong Bible Guide

1. **No Other Gods**
    "You shall have no other gods before me." - Exodus
    20:3

2. **No Idols or Images**
    "You shall not make for yourself an image…"
    (Worship God only) - Exodus 20:4

3. **Respect God's Name**
    "You shall not misuse the name of the LORD your
    God…" - Exodus 20:7

4. **Keep the Sabbath Holy**
    "Remember the Sabbath day by keeping it holy." -
    Exodus 20:8

5. **Love God Fully**
    "Love the LORD your God with all your heart and
    with all your soul and with all your strength." -
    Deuteronomy 6:5

6. **Jesus' Greatest Commandment**
    "Jesus replied: 'Love the Lord your God with all your
    heart and with all your soul and with all your mind.'"
    - Matthew 22:37

7. **Worship God Alone**
    "Worship the Lord your God, and serve him only." -
    Matthew 4:10

8. Trust in God Completely

"Trust in the LORD with all your heart and lean not on your own understanding;" - Proverbs 3:5

9. Submit to God's Guidance

"in all your ways submit to him, and he will make your paths straight." - Proverbs 3:6

10. Show Love by Obedience

"If you love me, keep my commands." - John 14:15

11. Love God's Commands

"In fact, this is love for God: to keep his commands. And his commands are not burdensome," - 1 John 5:3

12. Seek God's Kingdom First

"But seek first his kingdom and his righteousness, and all these things will be given to you as well." - Matthew 6:33

13. Meditate on God's Word

"Keep this Book of the Law always on your lips; meditate on it day and night, so that you may be careful to do everything written in it. Then you will be prosperous and successful." - Joshua 1:8

14. Hide God's Word in Your Heart

"I have hidden your word in my heart that I might not sin against you." - Psalm 119:11

15. **Submit to God, Resist the Devil**

"Submit yourselves, then, to God. Resist the devil, and he will flee from you." - James 4:7

16. **Draw Near to God**

"Come near to God and he will come near to you…" - James 4:8

17. **Rejoice Always**

"Rejoice always," - 1 Thessalonians 5:16

18. **Pray Continually**

"Pray continually," - 1 Thessalonians 5:17

19. **Give Thanks in All Circumstances**

"Give thanks in all circumstances; for this is God's will for you in Christ Jesus." - 1 Thessalonians 5:18

20. **Keep Meeting Together**

"…not giving up meeting together, as some are in the habit of doing, but encouraging one another—and all the more as you see the Day approaching." - Hebrews 10:25

21. **Do Everything for God's Glory**

"So whether you eat or drink or whatever you do, do it all for the glory of God." - 1 Corinthians 10:31

22. **Do All in Jesus' Name**
"And whatever you do, whether in word or deed, do it all in the name of the Lord Jesus, giving thanks to God the Father through him." - Colossians 3:17

23. **Work Wholeheartedly for the Lord**
"Whatever you do, work at it with all your heart, as working for the Lord, not for human masters," - Colossians 3:23

24. **Bring the Offering to God**
"Bring the whole tithe into the storehouse..." (Regarding giving) - Malachi 3:10

25. **Make Disciples of All Nations**
"Therefore go and make disciples of all nations..." (The Great Commission) - Matthew 28:19

2.2. Honoring Parents & Authority

God places a high value on **honoring parents** — so much so that He made it a commandment, one that comes with a promise of blessing and long life (Exodus 20:12). Whether you're a child, teen, or adult, **obeying, listening to, and respecting your father and mother** is a reflection of your heart toward God.

Verses in Proverbs remind us that listening to our parents' instruction and not ignoring their wisdom brings understanding and life. Even as they grow older, **respect and care for them is part of godly living** (Proverbs 23:22).

This call to honor doesn't stop with parents. **God wants us to respect all forms of authority** — including teachers, leaders, and government. Romans 13:1 and Hebrews 13:17 teach us that **submission is not weakness, but wisdom**, acknowledging that God is the One who ultimately appoints every authority.

When we obey with the right heart, we please God (Colossians 3:20), reflect His order and peace, and allow those in leadership — whether at home or in society — to lead with joy, not grief.

In-short:
Honor your parents. Obey with love. Respect authority. Please the Lord.

1.   **Honor Your Parents**
     "Honor your father and your mother, so that you
     may live long in the land the LORD your God is giving
     you." - Exodus 20:12

2.   **Children, Obey Your Parents**
     "Children, obey your parents in the Lord, for this is
     right." - Ephesians 6:1

3.   **Honor Commandment with Promise**
     "Honor your father and mother'- which is the first
     commandment with a promise" - Ephesians 6:2

4.   **Obedience Pleases the Lord**
     "Children, obey your parents in everything, for this
     pleases the Lord." - Colossians 3:20

5.   **Listen to Parental Instruction**
     "Listen, my son, to your father's instruction and do
     not forsake your mother's teaching." - Proverbs 1:8

6.   **Keep Your Parents' Commands**
     "My son, keep your father's command and do not
     forsake your mother's teaching." - Proverbs 6:20

7.   **Wise Son Hears Reproof**
     "A wise son heeds his father's instruction, but a
     mocker does not respond to rebuke." - Proverbs 13:1

8. **Respect Elderly Parents**

    "Listen to your father, who gave you life, and do not despise your mother when she is old." - Proverbs 23:22

9. **Submit to Authorities**

    "Let everyone be subject to the governing authorities, for there is no authority except that which God has established..." - Romans 13:1

10. **Respect and Support Your Leaders**

    "Have confidence in your leaders and submit to their authority, because they keep watch over you as those who must give an account. Do this so that their work will be a joy, not a burden, for that would be of no benefit to you." - Hebrews 13:17

2.3. Personal Character, Purity & Conduct

God cares deeply about who you are on the inside — your thoughts, actions, purity, honesty, and the company you keep.

1 Timothy 4:12 encourages us, no matter our age, to **lead by example** in everything: in speech, love, conduct, and faith. This call is not just for public life, but for **private purity** too. God's will for you is **to be holy**, set apart, guarding your heart and mind (1 Peter 1:15–16, Proverbs 4:23). That means saying no to sin, especially the sexual temptations and moral decay that surround us (1 Corinthians 6:18, Colossians 3:5).

To grow in purity, we must **renew our minds** daily with God's Word and focus on what is true and lovely (Romans 12:2, Philippians 4:8). The Holy Spirit works in us to bear fruit like love, joy, peace, and self-control (Galatians 5:22–23). So we **put off the old self** and put on compassion, kindness, patience, and integrity (Ephesians 4:22–24, Colossians 3:12).

Truthfulness matters. God detests lying and dishonesty, but He delights in those who are trustworthy (Proverbs 12:22). That's why we are commanded not to steal, lie, or deceive — but to speak the truth and work honestly, sharing with those in need (Ephesians 4:25, 28).

Our relationships shape our walk with God. The Bible warns against keeping company with fools, mockers, or angry people, because they influence us. Instead, choose wise and godly friends (Proverbs 13:20, 1 Corinthians 15:33).

Self-control, patience, and humility are more powerful than strength or status (Proverbs 16:32). And through it all, **treat others the way you want to be treated** — this is the Golden Rule (Luke 6:31).

In-summary:
Be holy. Be honest. Be humble. Be wise. Be set apart for God.

1. **Set an Example in Speech and Conduct**
   "Don't let anyone look down on you because you are young, but set an example for the believers in speech, in conduct, in love, in faith and in purity." - 1 Timothy 4:12

2. **Flee Evil Desires; Pursue Righteousness**
   "Flee the evil desires of youth and pursue righteousness, faith, love and peace, along with those who call on the Lord out of a pure heart." - 2 Timothy 2:22

3. **Be Holy Because God is Holy**

"But just as he who called you is holy, so be holy in all you do; for it is written: 'Be holy, because I am holy.'" - 1 Peter 1:15-16

4. **Think on What is Pure and Praiseworthy**

    "Finally, brothers and sisters, whatever is true, whatever is noble, whatever is right, whatever is pure, whatever is lovely, whatever is admirable - if anything is excellent or praiseworthy - think about such things." - Philippians 4:8

5. **Renew Your Mind; Don't Conform to World**

    "Do not conform to the pattern of this world, but be transformed by the renewing of your mind..." - Romans 12:2

6. **Flee Sexual Immorality**

    "Flee from sexual immorality..." - 1 Corinthians 6:18

7. **Avoid All Sexual Impurity**

    "But among you there must not be even a hint of sexual immorality, or of any kind of impurity, or of greed, because these are improper for God's holy people." - Ephesians 5:3

8. **God's Will is Sanctification**

    "It is God's will that you should be sanctified: that you should avoid sexual immorality;" - 1 Thessalonians 4:3

9. Guard Your Heart

"Above all else, guard your heart, for everything you do flows from it." - Proverbs 4:23

10. Fruit of the Spirit

"But the fruit of the Spirit is love, joy, peace, forbearance, kindness, goodness, faithfulness, gentleness and self-control. Against such things there is no law." - Galatians 5:22-23

11. Put on the New Self

"You were taught, with regard to your former way of life, to put off your old self... to be made new in the attitude of your minds; and to put on the new self, created to be like God in true righteousness and holiness." - Ephesians 4:22-24

12. Put to Death Earthly Desires

"Put to death, therefore, whatever belongs to your earthly nature: sexual immorality, impurity, lust, evil desires and greed, which is idolatry." - Colossians 3:5

13. Rid Yourself of Anger and Slander

"But now you must also rid yourselves of all such things as these: anger, rage, malice, slander, and filthy language from your lips." - Colossians 3:8

14. Clothe Yourself with Compassion and Patience

"Therefore, as God's chosen people, holy and dearly loved, clothe yourselves with compassion, kindness, humility, gentleness and patience." - Colossians 3:12

15. Do All Without Complaining

"Do everything without grumbling or arguing," - Philippians 2:14

16. Love Must be Sincere

"Love must be sincere. Hate what is evil; cling to what is good." - Romans 12:9

17. Be Like-Minded and Compassionate

"Finally, all of you, be like-minded, be sympathetic, love one another, be compassionate and humble." - 1 Peter 3:8

18. Honesty is Required

"The LORD detests dishonest scales, but accurate weights find favor with him." - Proverbs 11:1

19. God Delights in Truthfulness

"The LORD detests lying lips, but he delights in people who are trustworthy." - Proverbs 12:22

20. Put Off Falsehood, Speak Truthfully

"Therefore each of you must put off falsehood and speak truthfully to your neighbor..." - Ephesians 4:25

21. Work Honestly, Share with Needy

"Anyone who has been stealing must steal no longer, but must work, doing something useful with their own hands, that they may have something to share with those in need." - Ephesians 4:28

22. Do Not Steal or Lie

"Do not steal. "'Do not lie. "'Do not deceive one another." - Leviticus 19:11

23. Do Not Steal

"You shall not steal." - Exodus 20:15

24. Do Not Give False Testimony

"You shall not give false testimony against your neighbor." - Exodus 20:16

25. Do Not Covet

"You shall not covet..." - Exodus 20:17

26. The Golden Rule

"Do to others as you would have them do to you." - Luke 6:31

27. Bad Company Corrupts Good Character

"Do not be misled: 'Bad company corrupts good character.'" - 1 Corinthians 15:33

28. Walk with the Wise

"Walk with the wise and become wise, for a companion of fools suffers harm." - Proverbs 13:20

29. Avoid Hot-Tempered Friends

"Do not make friends with a hot-tempered person, do not associate with one easily angered, or you may learn their ways and get yourself ensnared." - Proverbs 22:24-25

30. Avoid Company of Mockers

"Blessed is the one who does not walk in step with the wicked or stand in the way that sinners take or sit in the company of mockers." - Psalm 1:1

31. Self-Control is Better Than Conquest

"Better a patient person than a warrior, one with self-control than one who takes a city." - Proverbs 16:32

2.4. Speech & Relationships

Love is the foundation of the Christian life.

Jesus said the second greatest commandment is to love your neighbor as yourself (Leviticus 19:18). He took it further by giving a new command: *"Love one another as I have loved you"* (John 13:34). That love even extends to enemies and those who persecute you (Matthew 5:44).

But love isn't just a feeling — it's seen in how we speak, act, and treat others. God calls us to speak with grace and gentleness, never tearing others down but always building them up (Ephesians 4:29, Proverbs 15:1). Our words can heal or harm — they should be like honeycomb: sweet and healing (Proverbs 16:24).

True love forgives. We're commanded to forgive others just as God forgave us (Ephesians 4:32). Even when wronged, we're to bless and not curse, to repay evil with good, and to live at peace as much as possible (Romans 12:14–18).

Unity and harmony are marks of the Spirit. We're to bear with one another in love, keep the unity of the Spirit through peace, and live in harmony, not pride or division (Ephesians 4:2–3, Romans 12:16).

We are also called to serve and uplift others: to encourage, carry burdens, rejoice and mourn with them, and pray for their healing (Galatians 6:2, James 5:16).

Jesus invites us to lay down judgment, offer forgiveness, and extend compassion and patience, just as He does with us (Luke 6:37).

In a self-centered world, God's people are called to live in a radical, sacrificial love — one that puts others first, speaks life, brings healing, and seeks peace.

1. **Love Your Neighbor**
   "Love your neighbor as yourself." - Leviticus 19:18

2. **Love One Another (Jesus' Command)**
   "A new command I give you: Love one another. As I have loved you, so you must love one another." - John 13:34

3. **Love Your Enemies**
   "But I tell you, love your enemies and pray for those who persecute you," - Matthew 5:44

4. **Graceful Speech**
   "Let your conversation be always full of grace, seasoned with salt, so that you may know how to answer everyone." - Colossians 4:6

5. **Avoid Unwholesome Talk**
   "Do not let any unwholesome talk come out of your mouths, but only what is helpful for building others up according to their needs..." - Ephesians 4:29

6. **Gracious Words Heal**

   "Gracious words are a honeycomb, sweet to the soul and healing to the bones." - Proverbs 16:24

7. **Gentle Answer Calms Anger**

   "A gentle answer turns away wrath, but a harsh word stirs up anger." - Proverbs 15:1

8. **Patience Demonstrates Understanding**

   "Whoever is patient has great understanding, but one who is quick-tempered displays folly." - Proverbs 14:29

9. **Love Covers Wrongs**

   "Hatred stirs up conflict, but love covers over all wrongs." - Proverbs 10:12

10. **Encourage and Build Up One Another**

    "Therefore encourage one another and build each other up..." - 1 Thessalonians 5:11

11. **Be Kind and Forgiving**

    "Be kind and compassionate to one another, forgiving each other, just as in Christ God forgave you." - Ephesians 4:32

12. **Do Not Repay Evil with Evil**

"Do not repay anyone evil for evil. Be careful to do what is right in the eyes of everyone." - Romans 12:17

13. Live at Peace With Everyone

"If it is possible, as far as it depends on you, live at peace with everyone." - Romans 12:18

14. Keep Unity Through Peace

"Make every effort to keep the unity of the Spirit through the bond of peace." - Ephesians 4:3

15. Bless Those Who Persecute You

"Bless those who persecute you; bless and do not curse." - Romans 12:14

16. Rejoice and Mourn with Others

"Rejoice with those who rejoice; mourn with those who mourn." - Romans 12:15

17. Do Not Judge

"Do not judge, or you too will be judged." - Matthew 7:1

18. Judge Not, Condemn Not; Forgive

"Judge not, and you will not be judged; condemn not, and you will not be condemned; forgive, and you will be forgiven;" - Luke 6:37

19. Confess Sins and Pray for Healing

"Therefore confess your sins to each other and pray for each other so that you may be healed." - James 5:16

20. Carry Each Other's Burdens

"Carry each other's burdens, and in this way you will fulfill the law of Christ." - Galatians 6:2

21. Value Others Above Yourself

"Do nothing out of selfish ambition or vain conceit. Rather, in humility value others above yourselves," - Philippians 2:3

22. Be Humble and Patient

"Be completely humble and gentle; be patient, bearing with one another in love." - Ephesians 4:2

23. Live in Harmony

"Live in harmony with one another." - Romans 12:16

2.5. Faith & Trust

Faith is the heartbeat of our relationship with God.

The Bible defines faith as the confidence in what we hope for and the assurance of things unseen (Hebrews 11:1). It's the invisible anchor that keeps us steady even when our eyes can't see the way ahead. Without it, Scripture says it is impossible to please God (Hebrews 11:6). Faith is not optional — it's foundational.

Trust in the Lord is more than a suggestion — it's a lifeline. He is the eternal Rock, unshakable and sure (Isaiah 26:4). And because He is trustworthy, we can cast all our anxiety on Him, knowing He truly cares for us (1 Peter 5:7). Whatever burdens weigh you down today — worries, fears, uncertainties — His shoulders are strong enough to carry them.

When life feels overwhelming or the future unclear, God's call is not to panic, but to be strong and courageous, for He promises, *"I will be with you wherever you go"* (Joshua 1:9). And in that same Spirit, He whispers, *"Be still, and know that I am God"* (Psalm 46:10). In stillness, we find strength. In surrender, we find peace.

Faith also expresses itself through prayer. Jesus taught us to believe when we pray, trusting that what we ask in alignment with God's will is already being answered (Mark 11:24). And the Holy Spirit helps us pray on all occasions, empowering us to intercede not only for ourselves but for all the Lord's people (Ephesians 6:18).

Finally, we are welcomed into God's presence with confidence. Because of Jesus, we can approach His throne of grace boldly, expecting mercy and help exactly when we need it (Hebrews 4:16). This isn't arrogance — it's childlike trust in a faithful Father.

1. **Faith is Confidence in the Unseen**
    "Now faith is confidence in what we hope for and assurance about what we do not see." - Hebrews 11:1

2. **Faith Pleases God**
    "But without faith it is impossible to please God..." - Hebrews 11:6

3. **Trust in the Lord**
    "Trust in the LORD forever, for the LORD, the LORD himself, is the Rock eternal." - Isaiah 26:4

4. **Cast Your Anxiety on God**
    "Cast all your anxiety on him because he cares for you." - 1 Peter 5:7

5. **Be Strong and Courageous**

"Have I not commanded you? Be strong and courageous. Do not be afraid; do not be discouraged, for the LORD your God will be with you wherever you go." - Joshua 1:9

6. **Be Still and Know God**
"Be still, and know that I am God." - Psalm 46:10

7. **Believe When You Pray**
"Therefore I tell you, whatever you ask for in prayer, believe that you have received it, and it will be yours." - Mark 11:24

8. **Always Pray in the Spirit**
"And pray in the Spirit on all occasions with all kinds of prayers and requests. With this in mind, be alert and always keep on praying for all the Lord's people." - Ephesians 6:18

9. **Approach God's Throne with Confidence**
"Let us then approach God's throne of grace with confidence, so that we may receive mercy and find grace to help us in our time of need." - Hebrews 4:16

3. Heavenly guide for Adults

100+ Bible Verses for Purposeful Living

3.1. Core Relationship with God

3.1.1. Faith, Trust, and Obedience:

Walking with God requires more than belief — it demands **trust**, **obedience**, and a heart that **seeks Him continually** through prayer.

The foundation begins with *trusting the Lord fully*, without leaning on our own understanding. *"In all your ways acknowledge Him, and He will make straight your paths"* (Proverbs 3:5–6). Trust means letting go of control — choosing to believe that God knows best even when we don't understand the circumstances.

Jesus echoed this when He said, *"Seek first the kingdom of God and His righteousness, and all these things will be added to you"* (Matthew 6:33). The goal isn't to chase blessings but to pursue the **Blesser**. When our hearts are aligned with His kingdom, everything else falls into place.

Obedience flows out of this trust. As Paul exhorts in Romans 12:1, we're called to **offer our bodies as living sacrifices**, setting ourselves apart for God's purposes. True obedience is more than hearing — it is doing. *"Be doers of the word, and not hearers only"* (James 1:22).

James also calls us to **submit to God and resist the devil**, drawing near to Him with confidence (James 4:7–8). That nearness to God is cultivated through a posture of humility, love, and spiritual discipline. *"Let us love one another, for love is from God"* (1 John 4:7). Obedience is not just duty — it is love expressed in action.

We are also called to **live faithfully in community and holiness**: *"Strive for peace with everyone, and for the holiness without which no one will see the Lord"* (Hebrews 12:14). Faith must affect our relationships — guiding us to live with integrity, peace, and grace.

This deep trust and obedience are sustained by a **lifestyle of prayer**. Paul writes, *"Do not be anxious about anything, but in everything, by prayer and supplication with thanksgiving, let your requests be made known to God…"* (Philippians 4:6–7). In prayer, our fears are exchanged for God's peace.

We're called to **pray without ceasing** (1 Thessalonians 5:17), to **remain watchful and alert** (1 Peter 4:7), and to **ask God for wisdom** when we need direction (James 1:5). He is generous and faithful — always ready to answer those who seek Him.

And prayer is also healing. James encourages us to *"confess our sins to one another and pray… that we may be healed"* (James 5:16). Prayer connects us not just to God but to one another — restoring, uniting, and strengthening the body of Christ.

In short, a faithful life is marked by a rhythm: **Trust God deeply. Obey Him fully. Seek Him constantly.**

When these three flow together — faith, obedience, and prayer — the Christian walk becomes not just a belief system but a vibrant relationship with the living God.

1. "Trust in the Lord with all your heart, and do not lean on your own understanding. In all your ways acknowledge him, and he will make straight your paths." - Proverbs 3:5-6

2. "But seek first the kingdom of God and his righteousness, and all these things will be added to you." - Matthew 6:33

3. "I appeal to you therefore, brothers, by the mercies of God, to present your bodies as a living sacrifice, holy and acceptable to God, which is your spiritual worship." - Romans 12:1

4. "But be doers of the word, and not hearers only, deceiving yourselves." - James 1:22

5. "Submit yourselves therefore to God. Resist the devil, and he will flee from you." - James 4:7

6.   "Draw near to God, and he will draw near to you." - James 4:8

7.   "Beloved, let us love one another, for love is from God, and whoever loves has been born of God and knows God." - 1 John 4:7

8.   "Trust in the Lord, and do good; dwell in the land and befriend faithfulness." - Psalm 37:3

9.   "Strive for peace with everyone, and for the holiness without which no one will see the Lord." - Hebrews 12:14

3.1.2. Prayer and Seeking God:

1.   "Do not be anxious about anything, but in everything by prayer and supplication with thanksgiving let your requests be made known to God. And the peace of God, which surpasses all understanding, will guard your hearts and your minds in Christ Jesus." - Philippians 4:6-7

2.   "Pray without ceasing" - 1 Thessalonians 5:17

3.   "...be sober-minded, be watchful." - 1 Peter 4:7

4. "If any of you lacks wisdom, let him ask God, who gives generously to all without reproach, and it will be given him." - James 1:5

5. "Therefore, confess your sins to one another and pray for one another, that you may be healed." - James 5:16

3.2. Personal Conduct and Character

The Christian life is not only about believing in God — it's about becoming like Him. This journey of transformation is marked by **wisdom, integrity, emotional maturity, wholesome speech, and moral purity**.

Wisdom and Discernment: Guarding the Inner Life

We are called to live with wisdom — not the kind that boasts, but the kind that flows from humility and reverence for God. **"The fear of the Lord is the beginning of knowledge"** (Proverbs 1:7), and true wisdom begins with a heart that honors Him.

Guarding our hearts is critical: **"Keep your heart with all vigilance, for from it flow the springs of life"** (Proverbs 4:23). The heart is where our thoughts, motives, and decisions take root. A wise believer discerns what is from God, testing every spirit (1 John 4:1) and holding fast to what is good (1 Thessalonians 5:21-22).

Wisdom is not just intellectual; it's practical. It shows up in good conduct, in choices made with **meekness and self-control** (James 3:13).

Integrity, Humility, and Self-Control: Reflecting Christlike Character

A transformed life reflects Christ in conduct, humility, and discipline. As Paul urges: **"Do not be conformed to this world, but be transformed by the renewal of your mind"** (Romans 12:2). That renewal is shown in how we treat others — valuing them above ourselves (Philippians 2:3–4) and clothing ourselves with humility (1 Peter 5:5–6).

Whether young or old, male or female, all believers are called to a life of **sobriety, reverence, and dignity** (Titus 2:2–6). This integrity isn't restrictive; it's liberating — it helps us flee youthful passions and pursue righteousness with a pure heart (2 Timothy 2:22).

We're also reminded to **put to death the old self** — anything impure, indulgent, or idolatrous (Colossians 3:5). For we are sojourners in a broken world, urged to **"abstain from the passions of the flesh, which wage war against your soul"** (1 Peter 2:11).

Managing Emotions: Anger, Anxiety, and Grumbling

Discipleship is emotional stewardship. God never says we won't feel anger or anxiety — but He commands us to **handle them wisely. "Be angry and do not sin; do not let the sun go down on your anger"** (Ephesians 4:26–27). Anger must be short-lived, not festering into bitterness.

We're also exhorted to **"do all things without grumbling or disputing"** (Philippians 2:14) — our attitude matters as much as our actions. And when anxiety presses in, Scripture gives us this balm: **"Cast all your anxieties on Him, because He cares for you"** (1 Peter 5:7).

Speech and Communication: Speaking with Grace

Words have power. Our speech should build up, not tear down. **"Let no corrupting talk come out of your mouths, but only such as is good for building up"** (Ephesians 4:29). In an age of fast words and hot tempers, the wisdom of James rings true: **"Be quick to hear, slow to speak, slow to anger"** (James 1:19–20).

Let our communication be thoughtful, patient, and filled with grace — for we reflect Christ not only in what we say, but in how we say it.

Sexual Purity: Honoring God with Our Bodies

In a world of moral confusion, God calls His people to **sexual holiness. "Flee from sexual immorality,"** Paul writes, reminding us that sin against the body is uniquely destructive (1 Corinthians 6:18). We are to **control our desires with honor**, not as the world does, but in sanctification and respect for God's design (1 Thessalonians 4:3–5).

Purity is not repression — it is worship. Our bodies are temples of the Holy Spirit. Therefore, we honor Him by what we allow, pursue, and practice.

Final Reflection:

To live wisely is to live intentionally — guarding the heart, shaping our character, managing our emotions, controlling our speech, and walking in purity. This kind of life is a testimony not just in word, but in witness.

Let us walk this path with daily surrender, trusting that God's Spirit empowers us to live not just for Him, but like Him.

3.2.1. Wisdom and Discernment:

1. "Keep your heart with all vigilance, for from it flow the springs of life." - Proverbs 4:23

2. "The fear of the Lord is the beginning of knowledge; fools despise wisdom and instruction." - Proverbs 1:7

3. "Who is wise and understanding among you? By his good conduct let him show his works in the meekness of wisdom." - James 3:13

4. "Beloved, do not believe every spirit, but test the spirits to see whether they are from God..." - 1 John 4:1

5. "But test everything; hold fast what is good. Abstain from every form of evil." - 1 Thessalonians 5:21-22

3.2.2. Integrity, Humility, and Self-Control:

6. "Do not be conformed to this world, but be transformed by the renewal of your mind..." - Romans 12:2

7. "Do nothing from selfish ambition or conceit, but in humility count others more significant than yourselves." - Philippians 2:3-4

8. Clothe yourselves, all of you, with humility toward one another, for "God opposes the proud but gives grace to the humble." - 1 Peter 5:5

9. "Humble yourselves, therefore, under the mighty hand of God so that at the proper time he may exalt you." - 1 Peter 5:6

10. "Older men are to be sober-minded, dignified, self-controlled, sound in faith, in love, and in steadfastness." - Titus 2:2

11. "Older women likewise are to be reverent in behavior, not slanderers or slaves to much wine." - Titus 2:3

12. "Likewise, urge the younger men to be sober-minded." - Titus 2:6

13. "So flee youthful passions and pursue righteousness, faith, love, and peace, along with those who call on the Lord from a pure heart." - 2 Timothy 2:22

14. "Put to death therefore what is earthly in you: sexual immorality, impurity, passion, evil desire, and covetousness, which is idolatry." - Colossians 3:5

15. "Beloved, I urge you as sojourners and exiles to abstain from the passions of the flesh, which wage war against your soul." - 1 Peter 2:11

3.2.3. Managing Emotions (Anger, Anxiety, Grumbling):

1. "Be angry and do not sin; do not let the sun go down on your anger, and give no opportunity to the devil." - Ephesians 4:26-27

2. "Do all things without grumbling or disputing," - Philippians 2:14

3. "Casting all your anxieties on him, because he cares for you." - 1 Peter 5:7

3.2.4. Speech and Communication:

1.   "Let no corrupting talk come out of your mouths, but only such as is good for building up..." - Ephesians 4:29

2.   "Know this, my beloved brothers: let every person be quick to hear, slow to speak, slow to anger;" - James 1:19-20

3.2.5. Sexual Purity:

1.   "Flee from sexual immorality. Every other sin a person commits is outside the body, but the sexually immoral person sins against his own body." - 1 Corinthians 6:18

2.   "For this is the will of God, your sanctification: that you abstain from sexual immorality; that each one of you know how to control his own body in holiness and honor..." - 1 Thessalonians 4:3-5

3.3. Relationships (Family, Church, Others)

At the heart of the Christian life lies relationship — not just with God, but with people. From our families to our churches and even to our enemies, God's Word teaches us that love, humility, and grace should govern all our interactions. Every relationship becomes an opportunity to reflect the character of Christ.

Love and Forgiveness: The Foundation of Every Relationship

Jesus redefined love with a new commandment: "Love one another as I have loved you" (John 13:34-35). This love isn't based on emotion — it is sacrificial, intentional, and holy. Paul reminds us that genuine love abhors evil and clings to good (Romans 12:9-10), and that "love is the fulfillment of the law" (Romans 13:8).

Forgiveness is equally essential. As God forgives us, we're called to forgive others freely (Colossians 3:13, Ephesians 4:32). This forgiveness, whether extended to friends or enemies (Luke 6:35), reflects the mercy we've received. Love without action is incomplete — "Let us not love in word or talk but in deed and in truth" (1 John 3:18).

Even our freedom in Christ is meant to serve others in love, not the self (Galatians 5:13). When we forgive, we heal. When we love, we fulfill God's greatest calling on our lives.

Family: A Sacred Stewardship of God's Design

God designed the family to be a living testimony of His truth and love. Whether parenting, marriage, or caring for relatives, each role carries a divine purpose.

Parents are called to train up children in the way of the Lord (Proverbs 22:6, Deuteronomy 6:6-7), not just in behavior but in values. Fathers are to discipline with love, not provoke (Ephesians 6:1–4). Mothers and older women are entrusted to mentor younger women, modeling self-control, love, and godly conduct (Titus 2:3–5).

Marriage is a picture of Christ's relationship with the Church — sacrificial, honoring, and holy. "Husbands, love your wives as Christ loved the church..." (Ephesians 5:25). "Wives, submit to your own husbands, as is fitting in the Lord" (Ephesians 5:22). These are not outdated roles but sacred callings that protect and strengthen the family unit.

Providing for one's household is not optional — it is a mark of authentic faith (1 Timothy 5:8). The family is a daily altar where God is worshiped through service, patience, teaching, and grace.

Church and Fellowship: Building One Body in Christ

The Church is not just a place; it's a people, a spiritual family called to build up one another in love. Hebrews urges us not to neglect gathering together, but to "stir one another to love and good works" (Hebrews 10:24–25).

Christian community is rooted in shared burdens, accountability, and honor. We are to carry one another's burdens (Galatians 6:2), honor spiritual leadership (Hebrews 13:17), and relate to one another with respect, recognizing each other as spiritual family — fathers, brothers, mothers, sisters (1 Timothy 5:1-2).

Conflicts are to be addressed with truth and grace: "If your brother sins against you, go and tell him his fault" (Matthew 18:15). Restoration and unity are central to the life of the Church.

Final Reflection:

Our faith is best expressed in relationship — not just through worship, but through how we love, forgive, raise our children, treat our spouses, and serve the Church. Each relationship is an invitation to demonstrate Christ to the world.

Let love be your foundation. Let forgiveness be your rhythm. Let family be your ministry. Let the Church be your fellowship.

"In all things, let Christ be your example."

3.3.1. Love and Forgiveness:

1. "A new commandment I give to you, that you love one another: just as I have loved you, you also are to love one another." - John 13:34-35

2. "Let love be genuine. Abhor what is evil; hold fast to what is good. Love one another with brotherly affection..." - Romans 12:9-10

3. "Owe no one anything, except to love each other, for the one who loves another has fulfilled the law." - Romans 13:8

4. "For you were called to freedom, brothers. Only do not use your freedom as an opportunity for the flesh, but through love serve one another." - Galatians 5:13

5. "Put on then, as God's chosen ones, holy and beloved, compassionate hearts, kindness, humility, meekness, and patience, bearing with one another and, if one has a complaint against another, forgiving each other..." - Colossians 3:12-13

6. "Be kind to one another, tenderhearted, forgiving one another, as God in Christ forgave you." - Ephesians 4:32

7. "Little children, let us not love in word or talk but in deed and in truth." - 1 John 3:18

8. "But love your enemies, and do good, and lend, expecting nothing in return, and your reward will be great..." - Luke 6:35

9. "For if you forgive others their trespasses, your heavenly Father will also forgive you..." - Matthew 6:14-15

3.3.2. Family (Marriage and Parenting):

1. "Train up a child in the way he should go; even when he is old he will not depart from it." - Proverbs 22:6

2. "Wives, submit to your own husbands, as is fitting in the Lord. Husbands, love your wives, as Christ loved the church and gave himself up for her..." - Ephesians 5:22-25

3. "Children, obey your parents in the Lord, for this is right. Fathers, do not provoke your children to anger, but bring them up in the discipline and instruction of the Lord." - Ephesians 6:1-4

4. "But if anyone does not provide for his relatives, and especially for members of his household, he has

> denied the faith and is worse than an unbeliever." - 1 Timothy 5:8

5. "And these words that I command you today shall be on your heart. You shall teach them diligently to your children..." - Deuteronomy 6:6-7

6. "Older women likewise are to be reverent in behavior, not slanderers, but sober-minded, faithful in all things, that they may teach what is good, and so train the young women to love their husbands and children, to be self-controlled, pure, working at home, kind, and submissive to their own husbands..." - Titus 2:3-5

3.3.3. Church and Fellow Believers:

1. "And let us consider how to stir up one another to love and good works, not neglecting to meet together..." - Hebrews 10:24-25

2. "Bear one another's burdens, and so fulfill the law of Christ." - Galatians 6:2

3. "Obey your leaders and submit to them, for they are keeping watch over your souls..." - Hebrews 13:17

4. "Do not rebuke an older man but encourage him as you would a father, younger men as brothers, older

women as mothers, younger women as sisters..." - 1 Timothy 5:1-2

5.   "If your brother sins against you, go and tell him his fault..." - Matthew 18:15

3.4. Work and Stewardship

Work and stewardship are not merely tasks or duties—they are sacred opportunities to glorify God, reflect His character, and serve others with purpose and integrity. The Bible teaches us that how we approach our labor and manage our resources reveals the condition of our hearts and our faithfulness to God's kingdom.

Diligence and Purpose in Work: Serving God in Every Task

Our work gains true meaning when we commit it to the Lord (Proverbs 16:3). Whether in small or great tasks, our efforts are not for human praise but for God's glory (Colossians 3:23-24; 1 Corinthians 10:31). This transforms ordinary work into worship.

The Apostle Paul encourages believers to be steadfast and immovable, always excelling in God's work (1 Corinthians 15:58). Excellence is not optional; it honors God when we present ourselves as approved workers, rightly handling His word (2 Timothy 2:15).

Every action, from eating to working, can glorify God when done with intentionality and wholeheartedness. This perspective shifts work from a burden to a calling, inviting God's blessing on our plans and labor.

Financial Stewardship and Generosity: Reflecting God's Heart

True stewardship extends beyond work—it includes how we handle the resources God entrusts to us. Scripture reminds us that it is more blessed to give than to receive (Acts 20:35), highlighting generosity as a cornerstone of Christian living.

Contentment paired with godliness is great gain (1 Timothy 6:6-8), teaching us to find satisfaction in God rather than riches. Yet, the rich are called to do good, be generous, and share willingly (1 Timothy 6:17-18).

Giving should be cheerful and voluntary, coming from a heart that delights in blessing others (2 Corinthians 9:7). Honoring God with our wealth and firstfruits demonstrates trust in His provision and acknowledgment of His sovereignty (Proverbs 3:9-10).

Final Reflection:

Work and stewardship are intertwined disciplines that reveal our faith in practical ways. Whether through dedicated labor or generous giving, God invites us to participate in His work and bless others. Our daily tasks and financial choices become acts of worship when surrendered to Him.

Commit your work to the Lord. Work heartily as if for Him alone. Be generous, content, and joyful in giving. In doing so, you reflect the heart of God and experience His abundant blessings.

3.4.1. Diligence and Purpose in Work:

6. "Commit your work to the Lord, and your plans will be established." - Proverbs 16:3

7. "Whatever you do, work heartily, as for the Lord and not for men, knowing that from the Lord you will receive the inheritance as your reward." - Colossians 3:23-24

8. "So, whether you eat or drink, or whatever you do, do all to the glory of God." - 1 Corinthians 10:31

9. "Therefore, my beloved brothers, be steadfast, immovable, always abounding in the work of the Lord..." - 1 Corinthians 15:58

10. "Do your best to present yourself to God as one approved, a worker who has no need to be ashamed, rightly handling the word of truth." - 2 Timothy 2:15

3.4.2. Financial Stewardship and Generosity:

1. "In all things I have shown you that by working hard in this way we must help the weak and remember the words of the Lord Jesus, how he himself said, 'It is more blessed to give than to receive." - Acts 20:35

2. "..Godliness with contentment is great gain," - 1 Timothy 6:6-8

3. "As for the rich in this present age, charge them not to be haughty... to do good, to be rich in good works, to be generous and ready to share..." - 1 Timothy 6:17-18

4. "Each one must give as he has decided in his heart, not reluctantly or under compulsion, for God loves a cheerful giver." - 2 Corinthians 9:7

5. "Honor the Lord with your wealth and with the firstfruits of all your produce..." - Proverbs 3:9-10

3.5. Comfort, Strength, and Hope

Life's trials and burdens can weigh heavily on our hearts, but God's Word offers profound comfort, strength, and unwavering hope. When we lean on Him, we discover rest for our souls and power to persevere through every difficulty.

Peace and Comfort in Trials: Resting in God's Presence

Jesus invites all who are weary and burdened to come to Him for rest (Matthew 11:28). His peace is unlike the world's—a deep, lasting calm that guards our hearts even amid turmoil (John 14:27). Like a loving shepherd, God provides for our every need, ensuring we lack nothing essential (Psalm 23:1).

When burdens feel too heavy, we can cast them on the Lord, confident that He will sustain us and keep us steady (Psalm 55:22). Courage is ours because God's presence never leaves us; He goes with us wherever we face life's challenges (Joshua 1:9). And even when the future looks uncertain, God's plans assure us of hope and prosperity (Jeremiah 29:11).

Encouragement and Perseverance: Strength to Keep Going

Trials often tempt us to give up, but the promise is clear: perseverance brings a harvest in due time

(Galatians 6:9). In the midst of hardship, we are called to rejoice in hope, remain patient, and be constant in prayer (Romans 12:12).

Facing difficulties with joy transforms our perspective, knowing that God is shaping our character through every test (James 1:2). Fear has no place in the heart of a believer because God empowers us with a spirit of power, love, and self-control (2 Timothy 1:7).

With Christ strengthening us, there are no limits to what we can endure and overcome (Philippians 4:13). Our hope is anchored in Him, giving us the resilience to walk victoriously through every storm.

Final Reflection:

God's comfort is real and His strength is sufficient for every challenge. When we bring our burdens to Him, He offers rest, peace, and hope that surpasses all understanding. Encouraged by His Spirit, we can persevere with joy, confident that He will sustain us until we reach the victory He has prepared.

Trust Him today — find your peace in His presence, your strength in His power, and your hope in His promises.

3.5.1. Peace and Comfort in Trials:

1. "Come to me, all who labor and are heavy laden, and I will give you rest." - Matthew 11:28

2. "Peace I leave with you; my peace I give to you." - John 14:27

3. "The Lord is my shepherd; I shall not want." - Psalm 23:1

4. "Cast your burden on the Lord, and he will sustain you; he will never permit the righteous to be moved." - Psalm 55:22

5. "Be strong and courageous. Do not fear or be in dread... for the Lord your God is with you wherever you go." - Joshua 1:9

6. "For I know the plans I have for you, declares the Lord, plans for welfare and not for evil, to give you a future and a hope." - Jeremiah 29:11

3.5.2. Encouragement and Perseverance:

1. "Let us not grow weary of doing good, for in due season we will reap, if we do not give up." - Galatians 6:9

2. "Rejoice in hope, be patient in tribulation, be constant in prayer." - Romans 12:12

3. "Consider it pure joy, my brothers, whenever you face trials of many kinds..." - James 1:2

4. "For God gave us a spirit not of fear but of power and love and self-control." - 2 Timothy 1:7

5. "I can do all things through him who strengthens me." - Philippians 4:13

4. Heavenly guide for Seniors (Age 50+)

100+ Bible Verses for Peace, Wisdom, and Legacy

4.1. Wisdom, Discernment, and Understanding God's Ways

Wisdom is a precious gift from God—one that leads us to live rightly, walk humbly, and follow His perfect guidance. As we seek God's wisdom, He generously provides understanding that lights our path and shapes our hearts.

Seeking Godly Wisdom: Ask, Fear, and Choose Wisdom

When we recognize our need, God invites us to ask for wisdom, promising to give generously without judgment (James 1:5). True wisdom begins with reverent fear of the Lord, embracing His commands and honoring Him forever (Psalm 111:10). It is from God alone that knowledge and understanding flow (Proverbs 2:6).

Surrounding ourselves with wise companions strengthens our walk, while folly leads to harm (Proverbs 13:20). The value of wisdom far exceeds that of gold or silver—its benefits are eternal and life-giving (Proverbs 16:16).

Understanding God's Guidance: Trust and Illuminate Your Path

Trusting God wholeheartedly means not leaning on our own understanding but acknowledging Him in all our ways (Proverbs 3:5-6). God lovingly instructs and guides us, keeping watch over our journey (Psalm 32:8).

His Word acts as a lamp, shining light in the darkness and making our path clear (Psalm 119:105). Even the simplest heart finds understanding through the unfolding of God's words (Psalm 119:130). When we ask God to teach us His ways, He unites our hearts with reverence and truth (Psalm 86:11).

Applying Wisdom to Life: Justice, Mercy, Humility, and Careful Living

Wisdom is not just knowledge—it demands action. God calls us to act justly, love mercy, and walk humbly with Him (Micah 6:8). Patience and the grace to overlook offenses bring honor and peace (Proverbs 19:11).

Heeding wise counsel and accepting correction lead us to maturity and discernment (Proverbs 19:20). The wise seek knowledge carefully, while folly only multiplies through foolish words (Proverbs 15:14).

Therefore, we must live intentionally—making the most of every opportunity with wisdom, especially in a world filled with challenges (Ephesians 5:15-16).

Final Reflection:

Wisdom is a divine treasure freely given to those who ask and seek God's guidance with humble hearts. It lights our way, guides our decisions, and shapes how we live.

Let us daily pursue God's wisdom, trust His direction, and apply His truth, so our lives reflect His glory in all we do.

4.1.1. Seeking Godly Wisdom

1. "If any of you lacks wisdom, let him ask God, who gives generously to all without reproach, and it will be given him." - James 1:5

2. "The fear of the Lord is the beginning of wisdom; all who follow His precepts have good understanding. To Him belongs eternal praise." - Psalm 111:10

3. "For the Lord gives wisdom; from His mouth come knowledge and understanding." - Proverbs 2:6

4. "Walk with the wise and become wise, for a companion of fools suffers harm." - Proverbs 13:20

5. "How much better to get wisdom than gold, to choose understanding rather than silver!" - Proverbs 16:16

4.1.2. Understanding God's Guidance

1. "Trust in the Lord with all your heart, and do not lean on your own understanding. In all your ways acknowledge Him, and He will make straight your paths." - Proverbs 3:5-6

2. "I will instruct you and teach you in the way you should go; I will counsel you with My loving eye on you." - Psalm 32:8

3. "Your word is a lamp for my feet, a light on my path." - Psalm 119:105

4. "The unfolding of Your words gives light; it gives understanding to the simple." - Psalm 119:130

5. "Teach me Your way, O Lord, that I may walk in Your truth; unite my heart to fear Your name." - Psalm 86:11

4.1.3. Applying Wisdom to Life

1. "He has shown you, O mortal, what is good. And what does the Lord require of you? To act justly and to love mercy and to walk humbly with your God." - Micah 6:8

2. "A person's wisdom yields patience; it is to one's glory to overlook an offense." - Proverbs 19:11

3. "Listen to advice and accept discipline, and at the end you will be counted among the wise." - Proverbs 19:20

4. "The discerning heart seeks knowledge, but the mouth of a fool feeds on folly." - Proverbs 15:14

5. "Be very careful, then, how you live—not as unwise but as wise, making the most of every opportunity, because the days are evil." - Ephesians 5:15-16

4.2. Enduring Faith, Trust, and Hope in Later Life

As we journey through the seasons of life, especially later years, enduring faith, deep trust, and unwavering hope become our anchor. These qualities sustain us through uncertainties and bring joy and peace that surpass all circumstances.

Steadfast Faith: Confidence in the Unseen

Faith is the foundation of our spiritual life—confidence in what we hope for and certainty about what we cannot yet see (Hebrews 11:1). Without faith, it is impossible to please God; we must believe in His existence and trust that He rewards those who seek Him earnestly (Hebrews 11:6).

Those who place their confidence in the Lord are like trees planted by streams of water—strong, flourishing, and unshaken by drought or heat (Jeremiah 17:7-8). The Lord is our strength and shield, our help in every trial, worthy of our heartfelt praise (Psalm 28:7). We are called to live by faith, not by what we see with our eyes (2 Corinthians 5:7).

Unwavering Trust: Casting Our Cares on God

When fear threatens to overwhelm us, we are invited to put our trust in God, our refuge and fortress (Psalm

56:3). Committing our ways to Him ensures He will act on our behalf (Psalm 37:5).

We can cast all our burdens on the Lord, confident that He will sustain us and keep us secure (Psalm 55:22). Experiencing God's goodness firsthand fills us with blessing and joy (Psalm 34:8). His steadfast love never fails, His mercies are new every morning, and His faithfulness is great beyond measure (Lamentations 3:22-23).

Living with Hope: Joy and Peace through the Spirit

God is the source of hope, filling our hearts with joy and peace as we trust Him. Through the Holy Spirit's power, our hope overflows and strengthens us daily (Romans 15:13).

God's plans for us are good—plans to prosper and not to harm, to give us a future filled with hope (Jeremiah 29:11). This hope is steadfast and sure because God's love has been poured into our hearts through the Holy Spirit (Romans 5:5).

Hope acts as an anchor for our souls, firm and secure, holding us steady as we navigate life's challenges (Hebrews 6:19). In all circumstances, we are encouraged to be joyful in hope, patient in affliction, and faithful in prayer (Romans 12:12).

Final Reflection:

In later life, faith that does not waver, trust that rests fully in God, and hope that anchors the soul provide unshakable strength. May we continually lean on God's promises, rejoice in His goodness, and embrace the future with confident hope.

4.2.1. Steadfast Faith

1. "Now faith is confidence in what we hope for and assurance about what we do not see." - Hebrews 11:1

2. "And without faith it is impossible to please God, because anyone who comes to Him must believe that He exists and that He rewards those who earnestly seek Him." - Hebrews 11:6

3. "But blessed is the one who trusts in the Lord, whose confidence is in Him. They will be like a tree planted by the water that sends out its roots by the stream. It does not fear when heat comes; its leaves are always green. It has no worries in a year of drought and never fails to bear fruit." - Jeremiah 17:7-8

4. "The Lord is my strength and my shield; in Him my heart trusts, and I am helped; my heart exults, and with my song I give thanks to Him." - Psalm 28:7

5.   "For we live by faith, not by sight." - 2 Corinthians 5:7

4.2.2. Unwavering Trust

1.   "When I am afraid, I put my trust in You." - Psalm 56:3

2.   "Commit your way to the Lord; trust in Him, and He will act." - Psalm 37:5

3.   "Cast your burden on the Lord, and He will sustain you; He will never permit the righteous to be moved." - Psalm 55:22

4.   "Oh, taste and see that the Lord is good! Blessed is the man who takes refuge in Him!" - Psalm 34:8

5.   "The steadfast love of the Lord never ceases; His mercies never come to an end; they are new every morning; great is Your faithfulness." - Lamentations 3:22-23

4.2.3. Living with Hope

1.   "May the God of hope fill you with all joy and peace as you trust in Him, so that you may overflow with

hope by the power of the Holy Spirit." - Romans 15:13

2. "For I know the plans I have for you," declares the Lord, "plans to prosper you and not to harm you, plans to give you hope and a future." - Jeremiah 29:11

3. "And this hope will not lead to disappointment, because God's love has been poured out into our hearts through the Holy Spirit, who has been given to us." - Romans 5:5

4. "We have this hope as an anchor for the soul, firm and secure. It enters the inner sanctuary behind the curtain." - Hebrews 6:19

5. "Be joyful in hope, patient in affliction, faithful in prayer." - Romans 12:12

4.3. Finding Peace, Comfort, and Strength in Challenges

Life often brings difficulties that weigh heavily on our hearts and minds. Yet, God promises a peace that the world cannot give—a deep, lasting calm that comes from trusting Him (John 14:27). When we fix our thoughts on God and rely on Him, He keeps us in perfect peace, even amid uncertainty and fear (Isaiah 26:3). Through prayer and thanksgiving, we can cast our anxieties on Him, knowing His peace will guard our hearts and minds beyond all human understanding (Philippians 4:6-7). We are never alone—God is present wherever His people gather, strengthening and comforting us (Matthew 18:20; Psalm 29:11).

In our toughest moments, God is our Comforter, ready to ease our burdens and bring joy even in anxiety (2 Corinthians 1:3-4; Psalm 94:19). Like a shepherd guiding His sheep, He walks with us through the darkest valleys, providing rest and reassurance (Psalm 23:4; Matthew 11:28). His promises sustain us, giving hope and endurance when suffering presses hard (Psalm 119:50).

Though we may feel weak and overwhelmed, God's strength is made perfect in our weakness (Philippians 4:13; Isaiah 40:29). When we place our hope in Him, He renews our strength, enabling us to rise like eagles, run without weariness, and walk without fainting (Isaiah

40:31). Our God is our strength and our song—our salvation and our praise (Exodus 15:2). Through every challenge, we are invited to bring all our concerns to Him in prayer, resting in His loving care and provision (Philippians 4:6).

No matter what challenges come your way, remember: God's peace, comfort, and strength are always available to you. Trust Him, lean on Him, and be renewed.

4.3.1. Receiving God's Peace

1. "I am leaving you with a gift—peace of mind and heart. And the peace I give is a gift the world cannot give. So don't be troubled or afraid." - John 14:27

2. "You will keep in perfect peace those whose minds are steadfast, because they trust in You." - Isaiah 26:3

3. "Do not be anxious about anything, but in every situation, by prayer and petition, with thanksgiving, present your requests to God. And the peace of God, which transcends all understanding, will guard your hearts and your minds in Christ Jesus." - Philippians 4:6-7

4. "For where two or three gather in My name, there am I with them." - Matthew 18:20

5. "The Lord gives strength to His people; the Lord blesses His people with peace." - Psalm 29:11

4.3.2. Comfort in Difficult Times

1. "Praise be to the God and Father of our Lord Jesus Christ, the Father of compassion and the God of all comfort, who comforts us in all our troubles, so that we can comfort those in any trouble with the comfort we ourselves receive from God." - 2 Corinthians 1:3-4

2. "Even though I walk through the darkest valley, I will fear no evil, for You are with me; Your rod and Your staff, they comfort me." - Psalm 23:4

3. "When anxiety was great within me, Your consolation brought me joy." - Psalm 94:19

4. "Come to Me, all you who are weary and burdened, and I will give you rest." - Matthew 11:28

5. "My comfort in my suffering is this: Your promise preserves my life." - Psalm 119:50

4.3.3. Strength in Weakness

1. "I can do all this through Him who gives me strength." - Philippians 4:13

2. "He gives strength to the weary and increases the power of the weak." - Isaiah 40:29

3. "But those who hope in the Lord will renew their strength. They will soar on wings like eagles; they will run and not grow weary, they will walk and not be faint." - Isaiah 40:31

4. "The Lord is my strength and my song; He has become my salvation. He is my God, and I will praise Him, my father's God, and I will exalt Him." - Exodus 15:2

5. "Do not be anxious about anything, but in every situation, by prayer and petition, with thanksgiving, present your requests to God." - Philippians 4:6

4.4. Gratitude, Joy, and Contentment

A grateful heart is the foundation of a joyful life. God's love is unfailing, and He invites us to enter His presence with thanksgiving and praise (Psalm 107:1; Psalm 100:4). When we cultivate a habit of giving thanks in all circumstances, we align ourselves with God's will and open our hearts to His blessings (Ephesians 5:20; 1 Thessalonians 5:18). Remembering God's wonderful deeds fills our hearts with praise and deep gratitude (Psalm 9:1).

True joy is found not in circumstances but in the Lord Himself. Rejoice always, for the joy that comes from God is our strength and sustains us through every season (Philippians 4:4; Nehemiah 8:10). In His presence, there is fullness of joy and lasting pleasure that the world cannot give (Psalm 16:11). Even when we cannot see Him, our faith fills us with an indescribable and glorious joy (1 Peter 1:8). The kingdom of God is marked by righteousness, peace, and joy, gifts of the Holy Spirit (Romans 14:17).

Contentment is a treasure that comes from trusting God's provision. Godliness paired with contentment is true gain, teaching us to be satisfied in any situation (1 Timothy 6:6; Philippians 4:11). When we release our grip on material things and trust that God will never leave us, we find peace and security (Hebrews 13:5). It is better to have little with righteousness than great wealth gained through injustice (Proverbs 16:8). Even simple rest is sweet when we live honestly and faithfully, reminding us that true peace comes from God, not abundance (Ecclesiastes 5:12).

As you walk in gratitude, joy, and contentment, may you experience the fullness of God's blessings and peace in your life.

4.4.1. A Heart of Thanksgiving

1. "Give thanks to the Lord, for He is good; His love endures forever." - Psalm 107:1

2. "Enter His gates with thanksgiving and His courts with praise; give thanks to Him and praise His name." - Psalm 100:4

3. "Always giving thanks to God the Father for everything, in the name of our Lord Jesus Christ." - Ephesians 5:20

4. "In everything give thanks; for this is the will of God in Christ Jesus for you." - 1 Thessalonians 5:18

5. "I will give thanks to the Lord with my whole heart; I will recount all of Your wonderful deeds." - Psalm 9:1

4.4.2. Abiding Joy

1. "Rejoice in the Lord always; again I will say, rejoice!" - Philippians 4:4

2. "The joy of the Lord is your strength." - Nehemiah 8:10

3. "You make known to me the path of life; in Your presence there is fullness of joy; at Your right hand are pleasures forevermore." - Psalm 16:11

4. "Though you have not seen Him, you love Him; and even though you do not see Him now, you believe in Him and are filled with an inexpressible and glorious joy." - 1 Peter 1:8

5. "For the kingdom of God is not a matter of eating and drinking, but of righteousness, peace and joy in the Holy Spirit." - Romans 14:17

4.4.3. Cultivating Contentment

1. "But godliness with contentment is great gain." - 1 Timothy 6:6

2. "I am not saying this because I am in need, for I have learned to be content whatever the circumstances." - Philippians 4:11

3. "Keep your lives free from the love of money and be content with what you have, because God has said, 'Never will I leave you; never will I forsake you.'" - Hebrews 13:5

4. "Better a little with righteousness than much gain with injustice." - Proverbs 16:8

5. "The sleep of a laborer is sweet, whether they eat little or much, but as for the rich, their abundance permits them no sleep." - Ecclesiastes 5:12

4.5. Leaving a Legacy and Mentorship

Living a purposeful life means intentionally passing on what God has taught us. We are called to carefully remember God's mighty works and share them with the next generations, so His faithfulness continues to be known (Deuteronomy 4:9; Psalm 145:4). Our legacy isn't just about ourselves but the impact we leave through our families and communities. Choosing to serve the Lord faithfully sets a powerful example for those who follow (Joshua 24:15). By guiding children in the right path, we help secure a future rooted in God's truth (Proverbs 22:6).

Passing on wisdom and faith is a sacred responsibility. We must openly tell the stories of God's strength and wonderful deeds to encourage others (Psalm 78:4). Jesus commands us to make disciples, teaching and baptizing so that His love and truth reach every nation—and He promises to be with us always (Matthew 28:19-20). Like Timothy, we are urged to be strong in grace and entrust what we have learned to reliable people who will continue teaching others (2 Timothy 2:1-2). Mentorship includes encouraging godly living and character, especially in guiding younger generations with love, respect, and kindness (Titus 2:3-5; Titus 3:1-2).

As you consider your legacy, may you be inspired to live with purpose, mentor with intention, and leave a lasting impact grounded in faith and love.

4.5.1. Living a Purposeful Life

1.   "Only be careful, and watch yourselves closely so that you do not forget the things your eyes have seen or let them fade from your heart as long as you live. Teach them to your children and to their children after them." - Deuteronomy 4:9

2.   "One generation commends Your works to another; they tell of Your mighty acts." - Psalm 145:4

3.   "Instead of your fathers will be your sons; you will make them princes in all the earth." - Psalm 45:16

4.   "But as for me and my household, we will serve the Lord." - Joshua 24:15

5.   "Train up a child in the way he should go; even when he is old he will not depart from it." - Proverbs 22:6

4.5.2. Passing on Wisdom and Faith

1.   "We will not hide them from their children, telling to the generation to come the praises of the Lord, and

His strength, and His wonderful works that He has done." - Psalm 78:4

2. "Therefore go and make disciples of all nations, baptizing them in the name of the Father and of the Son and of the Holy Spirit, and teaching them to obey everything I have commanded you. And surely I am with you always, to the very end of the age." - Matthew 28:19-20

3. "You then, my son, be strong in the grace that is in Christ Jesus. And the things you have heard Me say in the presence of many witnesses entrust to reliable people who will also be qualified to teach others." - 2 Timothy 2:1-2

4. "Older women likewise are to be reverent in behavior, not slanderers or slaves to much wine. They are to teach what is good, and so train the young women to love their husbands and children, to be self-controlled, pure, working at home, kind, and submissive to their own husbands, that the word of God may not be reviled." - Titus 2:3-5

5. "Remind them to be submissive to rulers and authorities, to be obedient, to be ready for every good work, to speak evil of no one, to avoid quarreling, to be gentle, and to show perfect courtesy toward all people." - Titus 3:1-2

4.6. Health, Well-being, and God's Provision

God desires for us to prosper not only in spirit but in body as well. Our health is deeply connected to the life and peace found in His Word (3 John 1:2; Proverbs 4:20-22). A joyful heart brings healing and strength, while despair weakens us (Proverbs 17:22). In times of sickness, we can call on God's people to pray in faith, trusting in His healing power and forgiveness (James 5:14-15). God is our healer, worthy of our praise and trust (Jeremiah 17:14).

God is our faithful provider who meets every need according to His riches and grace (Philippians 4:19). Like a caring shepherd, He ensures we lack nothing essential (Psalm 23:1). Jesus reminds us to trust God's care by observing how He provides for even the birds of the air, assuring us we are of much greater value (Matthew 6:26). When we honor God with our resources and live uprightly, He blesses us abundantly, filling our lives with His goodness (Psalm 84:11; Proverbs 3:9-10).

May this assurance encourage you to rely fully on God's healing power and generous provision, living with faith and gratitude each day.

4.6.1. Trusting God for Health

1. "Beloved, I pray that you may prosper in all things and be in health, just as your soul prospers." - 3 John 1:2

2. "My son, pay attention to what I say; turn your ear to my words. Do not let them vanish from your sight; keep them in your heart. For they are life to those who find them and health to one's whole body." - Proverbs 4:20-22

3. "A cheerful heart is good medicine, but a crushed spirit dries up the bones." - Proverbs 17:22

4. "Heal me, O Lord, and I shall be healed; save me, and I shall be saved, for You are my praise." - Jeremiah 17:14

5. "Is anyone among you sick? Let them call the elders of the church to pray over them and anoint them with oil in the name of the Lord. And the prayer offered in faith will make the sick person well; the Lord will raise them up. If they have sinned, they will be forgiven." - James 5:14-15

4.6.2. God's Provision

1. "And my God will supply every need of yours according to His riches in glory in Christ Jesus." - Philippians 4:19

2. "The Lord is my shepherd; I shall not want." - Psalm 23:1

3. "Look at the birds of the air: they neither sow nor reap nor gather into barns, and yet your heavenly Father feeds them. Are you not of more value than they?" - Matthew 6:26

4. "No good thing does He withhold from those who walk uprightly." - Psalm 84:11

5. "Honor the Lord with your wealth and with the firstfruits of all your produce; then your barns will be filled with plenty, and your vats will overflow with new wine." - Proverbs 3:9-10

4.7. Love, Relationships, and Community

God's greatest command is to love—first Him with all our heart, soul, and strength, and then others as He has loved us (Deuteronomy 6:5; John 13:34). Love is the foundation that holds every virtue together, calling us to be patient, kind, humble, and forgiving. True love is enduring and reflects God's nature living in us (Colossians 3:14; 1 Corinthians 13:4-8; 1 John 4:7).

Valuing relationships means sharpening and encouraging one another daily. We are called to forgive as Christ forgave us and to lift each other up in humility, recognizing that we are stronger together (Proverbs 27:17; Colossians 3:13; Ecclesiastes 4:9-10; Philippians 2:3).

Community and fellowship are vital for spiritual growth. Meeting together, sharing needs, and serving with wholehearted devotion strengthens our unity as one body in Christ. In all we do, we serve the Lord, who rewards our faithfulness (Hebrews 10:24-25; Romans 12:4-5, 13; Colossians 3:23-24).

May your heart be filled with God's love, your relationships enriched by grace, and your community a reflection of His perfect unity.

4.7.1. Loving God and Others

1. "You shall love the Lord your God with all your heart and with all your soul and with all your might." - Deuteronomy 6:5

2. "A new command I give you: Love one another. As I have loved you, so you must love one another." - John 13:34

3. "And over all these virtues put on love, which binds them all together in perfect unity." - Colossians 3:14

4. "Love is patient, love is kind. It does not envy, it does not boast, it is not proud. It does not dishonor others, it is not self-seeking, it is not easily angered, it keeps no record of wrongs. Love does not delight in evil but rejoices with the truth. It always protects, always trusts, always hopes, always perseveres. Love never fails." - 1 Corinthians 13:4-8a

5. "Dear friends, let us love one another, for love comes from God. Everyone who loves has been born of God and knows God." - 1 John 4:7

4.7.2. Valuing Relationships

1. "As iron sharpens iron, so one person sharpens another." - Proverbs 27:17

2. "Therefore encourage one another and build each other up, just as in fact you are doing." - 1 Thessalonians 5:11

3. "Bear with each other and forgive one another if any of you has a grievance against someone. Forgive as the Lord forgave you." - Colossians 3:13

4. "Two are better than one, because they have a good return for their labor: If either of them falls down, one can help the other up. But pity anyone who falls and has no one to help them up." - Ecclesiastes 4:9-10

5. "Do nothing out of selfish ambition or vain conceit. Rather, in humility value others above yourselves." - Philippians 2:3

4.7.3. Community and Fellowship

1. "And let us consider how we may spur one another on toward love and good deeds, not giving up meeting together, as some are in the habit of doing, but encouraging one another—and all the more as you see the Day approaching." - Hebrews 10:24-25

2. "How good and pleasant it is when God's people live together in unity!" - Psalm 133:1

3. "Share with the Lord's people who are in need. Practice hospitality." - Romans 12:13

4. "For just as each of us has one body with many members, and these members do not all have the same function, so in Christ we, though many, form one body, and each member belongs to all the others." - Romans 12:4-5

5. "Whatever you do, work at it with all your heart, as working for the Lord, not for human masters, since you know that you will receive an inheritance from the Lord as a reward. It is the Lord Christ you are serving." - Colossians 3:23-24

4.8. Reflecting on Life and Preparing for Eternity

Life is fleeting, and God calls us to wisely number our days so we may live with understanding and purpose (Psalm 90:12). As followers of Christ, we are encouraged to run our race faithfully, keeping the faith, knowing that a crown of righteousness awaits us in eternity (2 Timothy 4:7-8).

To live with Christ as our focus means embracing both life and death with hope—living fully for Him now, and trusting that to die is to gain eternal life in His presence (Philippians 1:21). We are God's handiwork, created for good works that He has already planned for us to walk in, fulfilling His purpose on earth (Ephesians 2:10).

Though our bodies return to dust, our spirits return to the God who gave them, reminding us that our true home is with Him forever (Ecclesiastes 12:7). May this truth inspire you to live intentionally, focused on the eternal hope we have in Christ.

1. "So teach us to number our days, that we may get a heart of wisdom." - Psalm 90:12

2. "I have fought the good fight, I have finished the race, I have kept the faith. Henceforth there is laid

up for me the crown of righteousness, which the Lord, the righteous judge, will award to me on that Day, and not only to me but also to all who have loved His appearing." - 2 Timothy 4:7-8

3. "For to me, to live is Christ and to die is gain." - Philippians 1:21

4. "For we are His workmanship, created in Christ Jesus for good works, which God prepared beforehand, that we should walk in them." - Ephesians 2:10

5. "The dust returns to the earth as it was, and the spirit returns to God who gave it." - Ecclesiastes 12:7

<u>Our Books (Printed / E-Books)</u>

1. ஒரு வருட வேத வாசிப்பு திட்டம்
2. One Year Bible Reading Plan
3. *சங்கீதமும் நீதிமொழிகளும்*
4. *சங்கீத புத்தகத்திலுள்ள ஜெபங்கள்*
5. *தமிழ் - வேதாகம மனப்பாட வசனங்கள் பாகம் 1*
6. *தமிழ் - வேதாகம மனப்பாட வசனங்கள் பாகம் 2*
7. Tanglish - Vedaagama Manappaada Vasanagal 1
8. Tanglish - Vedaagama Manappaada Vasanagal 2
9. Bible Memory Verses Volume 1
10. Bible Memory Verses Volume 2
11. Bible Coloring Books 01 Creation [Tamil, English]
12. Bible Coloring Books 02 Adam and Eve [Tamil, English]
13. Bible Coloring Books 03 Cain and Abel [Tamil, English]
14. Bible Coloring Books 04 Noah [Tamil, English]
15. *ஞாயிறு பள்ளி பாடங்கள் - தொடக்கநிலை - பாகம் 1*
16. Tanglish - Gnayiru Palli Paadangal - Thodakkanilai - Baagam 1
17. Bible Coloring Book for Sunday School Syllabus Beginners - Volume 1
18. வேதாகம தியானங்கள் பாகம் 1 40 லெந்து நாட்கள் [ஆசிரியர்: கிளாடிஸ் சுகந்தி ஹாசிலிட்]
19. வேதாகம தியானங்கள் பாகம் 2 40 லெந்து நாட்கள் [ஆசிரியர்: கிளாடிஸ் சுகந்தி ஹாசிலிட்]
20. வேதாகம தியானங்கள் பாகம் 3 - [25 கிறிஸ்மஸ் தியானங்கள். ஆசிரியர்: கிளாடிஸ் சுகந்தி ஹாசிலிட்]
21. வேதாகம தியானங்கள் பாகம் 4 [365 நாட்கள். ஆசிரியர்: கிளாடிஸ் சுகந்தி ஹாசிலிட்]

22. தம்பிரான் வணக்கம் 1578 [ஆசிரியர்: பழங்காசு சீனிவாசன், ஏசுதாஸ் சாலொமோன்]

23. தமிழ் பைபிள் 1714 பாகம் 1 (மத்தேயு முதல் அப்போஸ்தலருடைய நடபடிகள் வரை)

24. தமிழ் பைபிள் 1714 பாகம் 2 (ரோமர் முதல் வெளிப்படுத்தல் வரை)

25. ஒருவருட வேதாகமம் (தமிழ், English, Telugu, Kannada, Malayalam, Hindi)

26. ஒருவருட வேதாகமம் - சம்பவங்கள் நடந்த கால வரிசைப்படி (தமிழ், English, Telugu, Kannada, Malayalam, Hindi)

27. தமிழ் வேதாகம ஒத்தவாக்கிய விளக்கவுரை

28. அபிஷேகம் [ஆசிரியர்: Rev. Dr. A. பிரகாசம்]

29. என் வாழ்வில் தேவனுடைய கிருபை [ஆசிரியர்: Rev. Dr. A. பிரகாசம்]

30. தமிழ் இணைநிலை வேதாகமங்கள்

31. English Parallel Bibles

32. கர்த்தருக்குச் சித்தம் [ஆசிரியர்: Rev. Dr. A. பிரகாசம்]

33. சீகன்பால்குவின் ஓலைச்சுவடி பிரசங்கங்கள்

34. தமிழ் வேதாகம பழைய மொழிபெயர்ப்புகள்

35. விசுவாச ஜீவியம் [S. பரமானந்தம் ஐயர்]

36. அன்பின் ஜீவியம் [S. பரமானந்தம் ஐயர்]

37. தேவசித்த ஜீவியம் [S. பரமானந்தம் ஐயர்]

38. நீங்கள் இயேசு கிறிஸ்துவை அறிய வேண்டியது மிக மிக அவசியம் [S. பரமானந்தம் ஐயர்]

39. கிறிஸ்தவ கடவுள் யார் - அவர் எப்படிப்பட்டவர்?

40. இயேசு கிறிஸ்து யார் - அவர் எப்படிப்பட்டவர்?

www.ingramcontent.com/pod-product-compliance
Lightning Source LLC
Chambersburg PA
CBHW031300130726
47988CB00007B/2656